A REASON

FOR RHYME

A REASON

FOR RHYME

by

Eddie Morales

Contents

Introduction

Ever since high school, when our poetry class read *The Raven* and *The Canterbury Tales,* I have been hooked on poetry. In particular, I have been drawn to rhyming poetry.

There is something about rhyme that catches my ear and makes its way to my brain where it mesmerizes me to the point of wanting to write my own rhymes; and this is my first attempt at doing just that.

Edgar Allen Poe became my favorite poet and it was a challenge for me to learn as much as I could about the art of rhyme, of which I knew very little.

There are many rhyming forms yet at the time all I heard at poetry readings was non-rhyming poetry.

However, in listening to the members of the audience conversing, I kept hearing comments such as, "Whatever happened to rhyming poetry?" or "Doesn't anyone in America know how to rhyme?"

Well, I listened and wrote this book of mostly rhyming poetry in the hopes that rhyme will someday make a comeback.

A REASON

FOR RHYME

A Reason for Rhyme

I want my rhymes to weep and sing—
express nostalgia and desire;
 thrust fluid verses from the spring
which flood the gates of Dante's fire.

I want to sculpt my words of stone,
so each, when chipped, in fine detail,
may find a soul to spark its own,
and like Rodin's pure art, prevail.

I want to brush my verses faint
with hues from Autumn's falling tears,
and in Monet's own Garden paint
impressions of immortal years.

I want to hear the spraying foam
from where fair Venus rose above,
and from her footprints on the loam
see rise the rhymes of mortal love.

I want to tame my verses wild
the way the cowboy tames his steeds,
then ride into the sunset mild,
with lasso 'round my tumbling weeds.

I want to live in days of old,
when Nymphs and Muses plucked the heart,
and lit the torches brave and bold,
with fire from the rhyming art.

But most of all, I want to teach
all children in the here and now,
that all the forms are theirs to reach,
if masters verse to show them how.

For every dawn there's end of day,
and like the rest, I'll serve my time.
But rest assured, the world will say:
This poet gave his life to rhyme.

A Daughter

I gazed upon her newborn face
and witnessed eyes where stars roam free,
a shine the sun could not replace—
the tears that fell like rain to sea.

I mirrored eyes where stars roam free
and comets sprayed her constellation
with tails that trailed like rain to sea
to fire heaven's inspiration.

To light the newborn constellation
I weave my love with hopes and dreams.
dab numerous stars for inspiration
and polish well until it gleams.

I blend her love with hopes and dreams,
add smiles that no one can replace,
and cherish so the star that gleams
each time I gaze upon her face.

A Mortal Love

No Venus do I favor for my love.
All plinths are clouds, and Icarus knew late
The heavy humor of a man so far above
This fragile world where fluid wings tempt Fate.

On earthly soil my lady I await,
Where passion's eyes entreat the lips to meet
In whispered songs of mortal love that wake
The nature of the flesh—so frail and sweet!
And we will dance above the gods beneath her feet.

An Old Sailor's Lament

O'er spraying foam the seagulls roam,
far from the waves on shore.
Soft breezes cool this sun burnt fool
who knocks on Ocean's door.

Pulling fish net from out the wet
and unrelenting sea,
dull fingers ache, the hips near break,
from sheer propensity.

Rowing astern, rope muscles burn,
seagulls scream for the haul.
Faltering eyes squeeze fading skies
as Sun begins to fall.

Night's seadog breath sighs at Day's death,
moonlight caresses sand.
Through salty eyes this tar espies
the wretchedness of land.

Oh, Briny One! The day is done!
Where flew the Siren's song?
Strength far declined is so inclined
to take the ears along.

Beneath the foam sea maidens roam,
tomorrow, far from shore,
Deep Ocean cool this sun burnt fool
who knocks on Mercy's door.

Blight Within

You're like a vampish demon of the night
who proffers flesh from murky shadows deep;
you crave my core, where brightly burns the light,

and strike me with a mamba's deadly leap.
Incisors quickly move the juice on past
the threshold of my mind, so I fear Sleep.

But hear me! I will crush the dread and cast
us both upon the rocks of human strife,
where we will writhe until the very last!

Come fangs! Extract your pools of crimson life!

Blinding Light

Reveal your thoughts to me my blushing Rose.
What jealousy conspires to lose your face?
Why seek, Lily, to be a Moon, morose,
When being is eclipsed by greater Grace?
Why, Sun, are your rays so melancholy?
My Stars, what makes a radiant Orchid cry?
Oh, I know! She is the fire who burns wholly
The enamored heart, and catches the eye!
It doesn't matter, fickle Destiny,
These vain attempts to bring my pasture gloom,
Because you know I love her, and you see,
The Daisies are no lesser for their bloom.
Bless the Tulips wherein ever they grow,
And bless the woman whom I've grown to know.

Butterfly Dancing

My wide-eyed child and I know of colorful things
that dip and skim over summer hills and meadows,
of fancy freedom held aloft by wispy wings,
of frail, orange petals edged in ebon shadows.

From grassy beds, between Oaks and Weeping Willows,
my little garden walker and I greet the sky—
an azure floor sprinkled with fluffy white pillows,
all spot-lit by the yellow ball squinting the eye.

And the dance commences—a Monarch's pirouette!
Then a plié and rise on the breath of the breeze!
How my wide-eyed child laughs at the King's minuet,
while I smile at my heart soaring over the trees.

My wide-eyed child—where's the chrysalis you slept in?
When did the spark of spring melt down old winter snow?
Wise for spring not to tarry where my mind has been,
for summer craves the rainbow and the Monarch's glow.

My wide-eyed child—I know the wonders of your flight,
for I have seen the hills and meadows of my day.
Humbled is the breeze by the strength of your wings!
Dance by summer's light!
And I will keep our garden well, until my winter comes to
stay.

By Candlelight

I see the look of ecstasy
upon your face when we make love,
and wonder what you're thinking of,
when you sigh, smile, and kiss my lips,
caress me with your fingertips.

I feel the fire of your love
and your urgency for passion
when we knead and mold and fashion
legs and arms about each other,
while our dark light-figures hover.

I want to burn in your embrace,
hear your cries, feel you tremble,
as we tussle to resemble
the dance-moves of the breeze-blown flame
that casts our shadows without shame.
For that is how we want . . . and need . . . to love.

Death of a Hamster

Hampton, belly laced with gnawed wire mesh,
his renascent freedom quickly undone,
squeaks the dire weakness of his flesh,
from the prison cell his journey started from.

Hobbling, trembling limbs reveal strength declined,
while the fire within torments the flow of light;
and the crimson trail proves the metal quite unkind,
like a strike of lightning out of darkest night.

Tightly curled within curls of shaved wood,
eyelids slowly draping over eternity,
the rigor rushes in to do him good—
tortuous flames sway to death's serenity.

In a matchbox filled with trimmings from his bed,
the cadaver rests in the Eden he once sought,
underneath the oak leaves on the limbs overhead,
cradled in the cycle Life has wrought.

Desperate Times (Circa 1953)

Oh, cruel Life! You heave a heavy plow
Across Aguada, in Borinquen fair,
Where streaming beams embrace the dawning air,
And silver rivers soothe the seething brow.

Where noble Scarlet Tanagers in plume
Thrust their songs to maidens of the spring!"
Where mangoes, plump and plucked, or fallen, bring
To Sunday mart a vendor's desperate tune.

Where Juan entreats the Lord, "Hear my prayer:
Please sweeten their teeth for my sugar cane,
Make their bellies ripen for my plantain,
And ease, with coin, these moments of despair."

But such grants are rare—nothing like his shack!
Where Sara waits to catch his image in her eyes,
Where her womb is in blossom, like the seedling's rise,
And the coquí lauds the labors of his back.

Don't Give Your Land to Strangers Metal Cold

I

God, work done, resting on the seventh day,
Placed a soul upon the lips of the wind.
The wind descended, gathered ocean spray,
And kissed the land with breath of humankind.
The flesh did rise, it cradled in the nest,
Tended by the love of its kindred soil.
The land that yearly, by the sacred blest,
Offers up treasures to the sweating toil.
The land is truer than the heartless gold,
Don't give your land to strangers, metal cold.

II

Gaze upon the impassioned countryside,
The fine adornment of its purple hills.
Smell the aromas that on breezes ride,
The life springing up from the heaven-spills.
The loamy fruits enliven the frail mind,
They stoke the blood fires of the tilling heart,
Where pride sustains the spirit and its kind.
And if a stranger should ask you to part
with your kin-soil, cast out the snake so bold!
Don't give your land to strangers, metal cold.

III

From the fertile plains, the grandiose land yields
to the admiring stranger this rare dream:
The ripening corn gathers in the fields
To sing the song of its richness; the gleam
Of the wheat carries the eye to the sea;
The orchards stretch upward to grasp the sky
And the razor's advantage slices free,
To carve into the soul, and bleed it dry.
Ancient is the caveat often told:
Don't give your land, to strangers metal cold.

IV

Tree-lined beaches against the ocean's ear
Are awe-inspiring to the gulls in flight,
And dire temptations to the profiteer,
Who slithers to the shine of silver's light.
Your piece of garden is the beating heart,
Faithful compatriot, noble and true—
Your legitimate mark in heaven's art!
If you barter land, you coin country too,
And there bleeds the sign to the young and old:
Don't give your land to strangers, metal cold.

Dream Significance

Towards the Sun I shot an arrow
On its way it pierced a Sparrow
The Sparrow, dead, fell to the ground
Thank God my arrow's safe and sound

Fair Lady

Until you beg surrender,
Relished you will be.
And if defeat
Is not your game
Then you'll have ravished me!

Flawless Love

Immortal Love is god to mortal man,
And perfect, whether men believe or not;
And treads without restraint, or master plan—
In mask—until unmasked by fallen heart.
But changed is not the face behind the guise!
Oh no! Disclosure merely lights the love
Who takes Love's place, and catches blinded eyes!
And thereafter, such changes shake and move
The lover and beloved, evermore,
Through temperate and tempestuous days.
And in the end, when Time taps on their door,
Time's moved by Love's true never dying ways.
The mask of Love no eyelets may possess,
Yet flawless is its vision nonetheless.

Full Circle (Traditional)

Not a thing on Earth to Heaven rises.
No bird, not gold, nor any vesture worn,
but the soul…divested of its guises.

Wisdom strikes the man who realizes
finality is nakedness unborn—
for nothing of the flesh to Heaven rises.

Fleeting are the ways of earthly prizes,
for even they, when from the body torn,
leave the flesh divested of its guises.

Poverty is what the flesh despises.
But poverty is but an earthly thorn,
and not a thing on Earth to Heaven rises.

I'll make for my own sake my sacrifices
and seek to know myself as I was born…
for when my soul is freed of all its guises.

The soul who shares my laughter and my cries is
the one whom, upon my death, I'll come to mourn,
for nothing left on Earth to Heaven rises
but the boundless soul…stripped of all disguises!

Full Circle (for the Pulpit)

Nothing! Absolutely nothing on this sacred Earth to
Heaven rises!
No bird on widest wings, not the promises of gold, nor any
vesture worn,
but this most precious of all things—the soul!—divested of
its guises!

Wisdom strikes the heart of every honest, humble soul who
realizes
Finality, our transportation to the infinite beyond, is
nakedness unborn—
for nothing of the fragile flesh to Heaven rises!

Far too heavy and so fleeting are the ways of earthly prizes,
for even these inconsequential things, when from the body
torn,
leave the flesh divested of its guises!

Truly, when I pause to think about it, poverty is what the
flesh despises.
And this I've come to ask myself: What is poverty? It is but
an earthly thorn!
And nothing on this vast and mighty Earth to Heaven rises!

I've come to my reality, and make for my own sake my
sacrifices,
for I have seen myself within myself, and seek to know
myself as I was born…
for when my coach arrives, and my own soul is freed of all
its guises!

The soul who walks with me, prays with me, shares my
laughter, my cries, is
the one whom, upon my death, I'll come to mourn,
for nothing of the Earth, or left on Earth, to my Savior's
Heaven rises
but this precious, boundless soul—stripped of all disguises!

I Bid You Love

I bid you, Love, make whole the broken heart
firing faint half-beats to a fading tune,
And whose garden spoils like an aging rot
that means to thrive beneath a dark new moon.
What star does a one-wingéd angel pursue?
Such spirit clipped is light without shine,
And the soul cries, when the heart hangs askew,
Dark tears from the depths of blind love's decline.
Bring Heaven's lantern and mending with you,
And meld into one heart...one soul...the two.

Johnny and Rose

While Rose lies there, sound asleep,
In a slumber ocean deep,
(Makeup done in marble face)
Johnny feels a chilled embrace.

He brings his lips to kiss her ear,
Whispers words she longed to hear,
And on his knees, sheds burning tears,
Brewed one night from ice-cold beers:

"We were going awfully fast,
I didn't hear the car horn blast.
It was too late, I swerved hard right,
And here you are a broken light.

"I love you, Baby, always will.
I hate my heart is beating still!
And if the angels hear my cry,
They'll give to you my last goodbye."

The time has come to feed the ground,
All watch in silence, not one sound.
The dirt is tossed, his eyelids close,
He lets go of his shattered Rose.

Poem by the poet
Death by drunken driver.

Life's a Tick

Tick tock tick tock tick tock,
Unlocking sequence to life's rock.

Tick tock tick tock tick,
Crawling is fun and walking slick.

Tick tock tick tock,
Running by a logical clock.

Tick tock tick,
 Moaning beside a roaming stick.

Tick tock
Lowering rectangular block.

Tick.

Long Live the King

A monarch, powerless to do battle,
By proxy bids his legions play the war.
So, by my hand, swiftly steel swords rattle,
As the expendable eight turn the score.
My Knights are fearless, my Bishops driven,
My Rooks wreak havoc with the ranks and files!
So dutifully their lives are given,
To thrust! the mighty Queen those last few miles.
With King and Queen I seal the Black King's fate,
And with one final blow, I yell, "Checkmate!"

Love and Honey

Love is like honey sweetly dripping.
No bee engenders tastier dew.
Lovers: delight in digit dipping
and savor this nectar through and through.

No bee oozes delectable dew
like the daisy bathed in passion's mist.
To savor this nectar, across and through,
drink of the mead sweet life has kissed.

Like the daisy bathed in passion's mist,
Love emits feverish condensation.
Imbibe the mead sweet life has kissed
and favor the dew its consummation.

Love radiates keen condensation;
Lovers: revel in digit dipping!
Until the dew finds consummation,
Love is like honey, sweetly dripping.

Medusa's Love Song

Within Medusa's flesh and bone,
in Stygian darkness tucked away,
there beat a heart of chiseled stone.

It drubbed a song, a Gorgon tone,
in hopes mere mortal men might say
they loved Medusa's flesh and bone.

But no love burned to spark her own;
Athena's curse prevailed each day,
And plagued her heart of chiseled stone.

Then Perseus, son of Zeus, alone,
with shield in hand, had forged a way
to strike Medusa's flesh and bone.

Her writhing locks began to drone,
And hissed the way the vipers pray,
"Pleas-s-s-e, pierce this-s-s heart of chis-s-s-eled s-s stone."

In slumber's peace, the sword struck home;
No longer would she swish and sway.
In death Medusa's flesh and bone,
did love the chiseled heart of stone.

Merlin's Hourglass

Mark each grain of life, sand-timer.
Let fall each soul to the bottom of eternity,
Where dragon heads and crowns of kings
Mirror the heaven of their descent.

Your wise spells, Merlin the Rimer,
Reach far beyond the four corners of infinity,
Where all life ends, all life begins,
While your hourglass marks each event.

My Dear Jane Doe

You lie there dead and out of breath
upon a slab so cold.
And yet there screams a voice: "My death
has secrets to unfold!

"I fear no longer mortal pain
from words that slice the heart.
I bid you seek my Christian name
before the clues depart."

But Death knows death, he claims out loud:
"Your soul is mine to keep.
I found you lonely in a crowd,
and by my hand you sleep.

"In life you shed your kith and kin,
In thought you sought the blade,
In deed you chose a mortal sin,
And now I give you shade."

Now take your secrets to the ground,
the ones I'll never know,
and sleep you, damsel, safe and sound,
good nights my dear Jane Doe.

My Garden of Roses

The early morning sun provokes the eyes,
While warbling robins raise a waking tune,
To stir the soul to greet one's dearest lives,
In yawn, and stretch, like roses striking bloom.
And sweetly they do wake these essences of mine.
They rise above bold mountains—rocky, steep, and tall.
Leap across wide oceans—adding nectar to the brine.
Spread petals over windy vales, like oak trees in the fall.
And each and every morning, my garden stirs anew,
And nightly, my frail roses are safely tucked away.
May their auras never fail to glow the whole night through,
So I can dream, and pray to see, another light of day.

My Little Smile

That teddy is not made for girls of twelve.
But you have hopes, as pre-teens always do,
in front of a reflection made to delve
for all the secrets deep inside of you.

When will your womanly
attributes arrive?

They've yet to come!
But don't hurry!
Take your time!

That you'll become a woman is too true.
There will be changes, but I'll see no change.
Those womanly formations will not hide you—
no matter how you shape and rearrange!

I'm just afraid your eyes will change as well.
It's a girl's inevitability,
to trade Dad's image for another's spell,
and I must have the heart to let you see.

You've yet to grow. Don't hurry. Take your time.

No Fancy Casket

Who needs a fancy casket for a bed?
I'd say the living—not so the deceased!
So chic, the silver pillow for one's head;
The satin sheets, with corners tightly creased.
A lively thought bestirs a lusty romp,
Where one can kiss a cheek, or smack the cheeks,
To prove that one's awake and still can jump
And crush the lips—to spill until it reeks!
Remove the lid and make it queen or king.
Then test the springs, and laud their moaning sound,
Because the world will never hear them sing
Inside the coffin six feet under…ground.
Endowment of such gifts need steady course,
When one takes breath before the rotting corpse!

Poetry

Poetry travels through a blind man's eye,
Hears a mute girl's cry,
Tells the deaf boy why.
It rocks the mothers while the babies sing—
Poetry can do anything!

Poetry hurls the Earth around the Moon,
Freezes fire in June,
Plays a silent tune;
It gulps the sparrows creeping earthworms bring—
Poetry can do anything!

Poetry mends with invisible thread,
Turns an oyster's bed,
Wakes the sleeping dead;
It scrapes off ships that to barnacles cling—
Poetry can do anything!

Poetry roars into a lion's ear,
Makes the fearless fear,
Makes the tearless tear;
It grows wild flowers from a mattress spring—
Poetry can do anything!

And Poetry's the Poet's beating heart,
His mind's work of art,
Her soul's counterpart;
But the greatest thing about all this fuss
is that Poetry—is all about us!

Reply to the Hummingbird

I
Don't let the rage within your heart
Conspire to turn it into stone
Far better when the heart's alone
To give oneself a brand-new start
If strewn about pick up each part
Serenely place them in my keep
My hand will wipe the tears you weep,
My kiss reverse the devastation
Healing the scars of my creation
Our love will flow like rivers deep.

II
The sorrow from your heart must flee
As our souls meld in sweet caress
And fan the flames of blessedness
To heights beyond reality
Close your eyes and you will see
The time is past for lamentation
I'll give you cause for celebration
Divest my flesh and at my core
Is what you seek and which I store
Love...beyond imagination!

III
My noble gesture misconstrued
Has caused you, love, to feel forlorn
Though reasoned well our hearts were torn
And by my absence did seclude
The life I hungered to include
Within the realm of my affection
I'll not take your soul's reflection
Your will to live enmeshes mine
Remember through the end of time
I'll always treasure love's perfection.

IV
With thunder and lightning's dissipation
Each trembling leaf dares show its face
The downpour cannot keep its pace
Tempestuous winds give resignation
Having survived annihilation
The Hummingbird insists anew
To seek the nectar flowers brew
So let us drink of Nature's wine
And bring our arms to intertwine
Until our lips taste love for two.

V
Two hearts have come to seamless blend
No limits do our souls proclaim
The human touch ignites the flame
That passion seeks not to contend
Or greater fire one must expend
To hide what hidden should not be
Do not repress your love for me
Let it take root and give it room

To face the sun in flowery bloom
No longer you . . . nor I . . . but we.

Sometimes Love

Sometimes love strikes like a cat
Pouncing on its prey.
It leaps, lands, claws your soul,
then shreds your heart away.

Once its belly is sated
Love calmly departs,
to seek another fool
to add to broken hearts.

Tetrad of Sonnets One: Passion

I – I

Beginnings

The spark that lights the heart inflames the eye
with sparkle stars must envy and adore.
This sight of love-at-first brings passion nigh,
and scorches every lover to their core.
Thereafter, lover and beloved dance
as one—in touch, in sight, in lips consumed.
The Moon is ever brighter for romance,
The Sun resplendent, flowers more perfumed.
Such splendid agony when all is new!
The agony! when fingers long to touch!
And lovers must imbibe their lover's brew,
For in that nectar, Life has poured so much.
Beginnings know that passion must begin
When sparkling eyes reveal the fire within.

I – II

Prelude to an End

How quickly fades a lover's dazzling light!
A lantern, lit by passion, must be fed
Continuously! Kept forever bright!
Or with the night, the light of day is dead.
Communication is the key to love:
With words a body writes without a word;
With smiles that make a lover pause and move;
With torrid eyes that hunger to be heard;
While listening is lock to hold the key!
But somehow, lover and beloved fail
To burn as one; and neither hear nor see
the agony their ailing lights entail.
The flicker of a flame begins to fade
When passion begs for Life, but Death is paid.

I – III

Endings

Such sadness veils those fallen out of heart
When sparkling eyes, so dimmed by passion's death,
Reclaim first sight, and lovers tear apart
With every deed that once gave love its breath.
A soothing touch turns crawling under skin.
The image in one's eye turns sight opaque.
A kiss transforms to ash the flame within
and heading back finds sealed all paths you take.
Are lost the days of sunshine and the moon?
It seems they go the way of day and night,
For roads too wide must fork, and all too soon,
thereafter, comes the dimming of the light.
An ending brings a chill to flood one's core
When passion dies and burns love's flame no more.

I – IV

New Beginnings

The Phoenix and the Flame are kindred souls,
And strangers not to Passion's burning depths.
The Sun, though dead by night, again consoles
The world at morning time, with newborn breaths.
So why not find Beloved flame anew?
Or Lover, find another source of light?
Perchance, relight the embers Passion knew,
And keep familiar lanterns burning bright?
Un-fork the road behind or move along!
But waste no time! For Time is quick to fly!
Rely upon the ember's crackling song!
And burn a sparkle in a lover's eye!
To burn away is Passion's sole desire,
When lovers, like the Phoenix, love the fire.

Tetrad of Sonnets Two: Hands

II – I

Baby Hands

A newborn needs no reason to exist
Except the reason Life's compelled to give.
Its hand, so frail, disposed to make a fist,
Appears to say, "I have a right to live!"
And both will cling to mother's soothing breast
By instinct than by knowledge of the act.
With time, these hands advance, are put to test.
In grasping, they inspect what hands attract.
They catch a fall; they grip another's hand,
Or set to rest if nothing goes their way.
They must be held if danger's in command
And made to stretch at length when safe to play.
Such fragile hands will learn of fists and prayer,
When knowing hands are called to take them there.

II – II

Hands of Youth
Adventure is the life of youthful hands—
Exploring all that needs to be explored!
They roil the waters, make their own demands,
And every step's a challenge to be scored.
If failure slaps the hands that stray too far,
The peaceful breast may soothe them once again;
But settled hands know where to set the bar—
So youthful ones find comfort from their pain—
So newly armed, and venturing anew,
They vanquish all that troubled them before.

The clock is always ticking Time's ado,
And hands, still soft, have yet to do much more.
O hands of youth! How fast you slip away!
When Time's own pulse beats down the light of day.

II – III

Mature Hands
Ah, settled hands, caress a youthful face.
Embrace, with ring upon your finger—Love.
Bethink, in times of woe, a joyful place,
Of moments held in prayer, of Saints to move.
Release from mind and heart the angered fist;
Discard the weapon War needs to survive.
Be gentle, when your essences insist
On holding own; act quickly to forgive.
Collect all petals fallen on the mind;
Reveal them when familial moments rise.
And keep, at hand, all friendships you may find,
For they hold cures for pain and tearful eyes.
The well-aged hands, and hands of youth, are blest
When those between them both, by love, are pressed.

II – IV

Well-Aged Hands

These hands have served their younger master well,
But Life soon leads them over golden pond,
Where, like the baby's hands, their frailties tell;
Where youth, now wrinkled, shriveled, and beyond
Repair, is petal precious on the mind.
But nobler hands await them in the end—
All knowing Hands, that well-aged hands will find,
Who care not whether theirs are slow to bend,
or ever walk another mortal strand.
For first, a soul's let go to find its birth,
and in return, must grasp the Lord's fair hand
Anew, and loosen memories of Earth.
Eternal are the gifts of love and grace,
When hands, unbound, touch God's immortal face.

The Death of Karetta Tress

The evil Lord Na-Tass, one moonless night,
From deep within the flames that Helkron wrought,
Flung forth a fearsome phantom spurred by light
That to the cradle maiden loins have brought.
Too late, when gone, a mother's soul delight,
That nine months kept in womb then proves has naught.
For when a child not blessed by water sleeps:
The spirit thief Karetta Tress there creeps!

But Jaho Vesh, great Lord of Haven-Or,
Sent forth the mighty wizer Axxon Thorn
To slay the demon lesser men abhor.
Within her den, by sacred sword well worn,
Her heart was pierced and from the body torn.
In Helkron's fires Karetta Tress will creep.
Fair mothers—bless the little souls to sleep!

The Flame

The moth and I have equal plight
We take to flight
To seek the flame
That sears the frame
With ever heightening delight.

The moth continues its endeavor
Far from clever
The landing's quick
And in a tick
Poor moth is doomed and gone forever.

To burn in ecstasy is swell
But know the spell
To quench desire
Fight fire with fire
So that the flame's consumed as well.

The King Who Would Be Jester

If love should strike a noble king
The symptoms could prove quite perverse.
His blue blood could flow in reverse.
Or worse, he might be brought to spring,
Much like a puppet on a string,
Or like a yo-yo, here and there,
So that his brain begins to wear
From the virus love injected.
Once his malady's corrected
Love will release him to despair.
For once he's cured and all alone—
Love's put the jester on his throne!

Tribute to Edgar Allan Poe
1809 - 1849

One of my favorite poems is Edgar Allan Poe's *The Raven*.
 I have read it over a hundred times and I enjoyed it as
much the last time I read it as I did the first time. It is a
haunting poem and its rhyme and rhythm always captivate
me from beginning to end. The last time I read it, an idea
occurred to me at the end of the poem. I thought the poem
was not finished. Of course, the poem is complete as is,
but what if, I thought, Poe had decided to write a sequel to
this poem. Parodies have been done of *The Raven*, but has
anyone done a sequel? This was my crazy idea—
to write a sequel. It begins exactly where Poe left off.

The Murder of Ravens

While my sorrow kept me weeping, Time stepped up his
painful creeping,
'Til the chariot of Apollo swept o'er the Night's Plutonian
shore!
And the Raven, never flitting, on the bust of Pallas sitting,
Like a viper, venom spitting, struck me once more to the
core!
Oh, how he made me shudder, the Raven o'er my chamber
door—
Still insisting: "Nevermore!"

But the nightmare mist departed, leaving mind and ear
unclouded,
And I heard a song that started from beneath the tufted
floor.
I began raving and ranting—like a banshee, wildly panting!
I felt nothing more enchanting than the voice of sweet
Lenore!
"Come to me!" I shrieked, "fair maiden, whom the angels
name Lenore!
Mute the Raven's, 'Nevermore!'"

Then a voice, like some bright candle, burned, "Take pistol
by the handle,
And blast! that wretched demon sitting just above thy
chamber door!
Leave no evidence whatever he sat there like blackened
leather,
Traces leave thee not one feather of that brazen bird of
yore!
Pluck the life, like feathers plucked are, from that brazen
bird of yore!
Quash the Raven's, 'Nevermore!'"

(Hark!) A deeper voice erupted, from some depth not yet corrupted,
And alarmingly instructed: (Leave well the pure and chaste Lenore!
Do not seek to make un-sainted, by this deed, so vile and tainted,
That which God so brightly painted, pressing doom to split thy door!
Grim and grave are plots engraved upon the Night's Plutonian shore!
Heed the Raven's, "Nevermore!").

Here the Raven, bird_and_devil, raised the note another level,
By pouring sanguinary evil o'er that one word I abhor!
"Prophet!" said I, "falsely praying!—death's a deadly game worth playing!
Keep thy blackened blood from spraying o'er my bust and chamber door!
Perch off the pallid bust of Pallas just above my chamber door!"
My Raven dared, "Nevermore!"

Then, the voice, with fiercer goading, set my flaming mind exploding!
Too, I dared not stop, and loaded lead and heart into the war;
While my maiden's song climbed higher, stared I red Raven-eyes of fire,
And heard a deeper voice suspire, (Now, doomed thou art, forevermore).
Still, the Raven, blasted Raven! that one last word did outpour!
The Raven croaked, "Nevermore!"

Settled by the madness broken, echoed I that last word spoken:
"Nevermore," said I, "dark token, from the Night's Plutonian shore,
Shall thy bolted beak torment me, or thy breast and breath present me,
With the word that now hath sent thee to the shadows on my floor.
Hallowed art thou, King of Shadows, by ebon hollows on my floor,
Longing for thy, 'Nevermore.'

"Fleeing sharp and cruel master lent thee far greater disaster,
When steadfast, Fate followed faster than thy wings could e'er outsoar!
From the east, now hear my Maiden, from within the distant Aidenn,
Balm she brings for me to bathe in 'til I feel the pain no more.
And the melody Fate guides now is the song of sweet Lenore!
Where croaks now thy, 'Nevermore?'"

Question asked, reply is certain—burning through each purple curtain,
Sun's light fired all and paled the ebon shadows on my floor!
Like the thunder, Lenore chanted, while the Maelstrom puffed and panted,
And my bones were newly planted in the horrors I once bore!
Bone for bone, one must atone, and I alone my terrors bore!
There, I whispered, "Nevermore."

Hammered by the hellish howling, grander demons felt I prowling,
Waiting, sniffing, drooling—growling! for the flesh my neck bones wore!
Though my mind the worst lay fearing, from my window I stood peering,
Keeping eyes upon the clearing, seeking sight of sweet Lenore!
Amidst the sea of marble stones—peering back stood sweet Lenore!
Then, I cried out, "Nevermore!"

Startled by this vile word spoken, somehow, found I, my voice broken.
"Doubtless," thought I, "what I uttered, came from weathered voice made sore!"
"Corvus! Darling!" called my maiden! "Say 'tis true you come to Aidenn!
Ever shall we be and bathe in Gilead's balm forevermore?"
Here I tried to make reply and tell her, "Yes— forevermore!"
Instead I cried, "Nevermore!"

Then, from beyond the marble sea, a thousand voices r-r-rocked for me,
And plied my maiden's agony, so twisted in the face she wore!
Greater pain my mind fermented, while that word Lenore lamented,
Knowing well my voice had sent it, and still I tried to speak once more!
I gathered deeper voice, to clear my voice—save! my voice once more!
Again I cried, "Nevermore!"

A thousand voices r-r-rocked for me, and from beyond the marble sea,
A plume, as black as black can be, rose high above the stone laced shore;
But 'twas no_plume_released that day, 'twas plumage from a higher sway,
Sent out to right, without delay, the blood I spilled moments before.
And while Lenore, "Oh, Corvus!" cried, I bid_adieu_to sweet Lenore
by crying out, "Nevermore!"

An Angel, with that word, alit beside the angel Life once writ,
And with Nepenthe's light relit the grimly, gravely pained Lenore!
The three-tier-wingéd Seraph drew Lenore into its arms and flew
Into a sky of Heaven-Blue, high above the stone-laced shore!
While then I prayed Lenore forget, once high above the stone-laced shore,
I ever said, "Nevermore!"

Anew, the voices r-r-rocked for me, and from above the marble sea,
Each puff of plume slid down to see restored the Night's Plutonian shore!
Like a canvas, feather tainted, puffs of plume the blue repainted,
With a sorrow well acquainted with the darkness my soul wore!
But no darkness could e'er blacken my bright vision of Lenore!
Though I'd see her, nevermore!

While gliding o'er the marble sea, again the voices r-r-rocked for me,
And from my window I did see a thousand ravens o'er Night's shore!
One by one, with flirt and flutter, every tree they sought to clutter,
While I pondered how to utter, "Please forgive me, sweet Lenore!"
But well I knew that word from hell, and_thought_instead, forevermore,
To torment her, nevermore!

Again, the ravens r-r-rocked for me—from every ghastly, purple tree!
And a thousand pairs of eyes of red lit up the frightening shore!
But_I_feared nothing, black or red! for Death cannot the dead un-bed!
And 'twas the living word I said that brought to me my sweet Lenore!
And the one soul_I_adore! shall fly with angels, evermore!
She flies!—so freed by, "Nevermore!"

And still the ravens r-r-rock for me, while here I rock eternally,
For I am King! of all the shadows on the Night's Plutonian shore!
And should you gaze into my eyes, therein a radiant maiden flies,
With no memory that my cries are all for her—my love Lenore.
And her love shall light my sorrow, morrow after morrow, and evermore.
I shall forget her—"NEVERMORE!"

The Rise and Fall of the Dark Angel

Part I: Satan's Ascent into Power

The Devil wields an army's dread
When hell-spawned hordes infest mankind,
And deviant spirits so inclined
Make dance at Satan's birthing bed.
Atrocities and curses spread
A crimson ooze to plague each nation,
Drowning all in trepidation,
For like a dream, these scenes unfold,
And not one prayer is left to hold
The certainty of our damnation.

Seven sins pervert creation,
Commencing with the thirst for gold;
With all good brethren dearly hold,
Demon eyes engorge their station;
Traps and flesh swell up temptation,
'Til the heart of light is broken.
Words of calling vilely spoken
Lead poisoned minds to favor sin,
And cast to wretched souls within
Anathema for a token.

The jaded man will quickly feed
Upon the Dark Heart's fetid chum,
And tear the flesh for goods and come
To cane his kith and kin to bleed,
Then towards his brethren plant the seed
So honesty puts up reverse.
His bride incurs a frenzied curse,
When her hearth is torn asunder,
By Black Lightning's coupled thunder,
And progeny spring forth perverse.

The good man leads his rib astray,
His rib then horns her tarnished crown,
And in dishonor's waters drown,
For wicked is the game they play
Before the trail that leads the way
Towards the land of false salvation,
Where the Sabbath's dissipation
Moves all to take the Lord in vain,
In front of idols held profane,
Blotting our Illumination.

The star lights fade from heavens high,
The moon no longer moves the sun,
Nor does man's soul reflect the Son;
For all that's good will come to die
In one last heaving anguished sigh,
As shrouds of darkness swallow light,
And give the demons vested might
To torment the sightless creatures
That once favored divine features,
But lost, find Satan rules the night.

Lo! Satan reigns one thousand years,
One millennium flood with tears.

The Rise and Fall of the Dark Angel

Part II: The Fall of Satan

From the eye of Satan's passion
There bursts a womb with blessed child.
The Lamb who fires the meek and mild,
Forging flesh in sainted fashion,
While the angel tears impassion
The Sword to spread his wings anew,
And fly into the Devil's brew
As silently as night is dark—
Retrieve the child and then embark
Upon the journey pure and true.

The child unveils the path to take,
As armies rise to heed the call,
To bid by grace all demons fall,
For from pure hearts true light will break
And through their eyes the bright souls make
The wicked rue their evil ways.
Beware! Here lie the crucial days,
As life and death are intertwined
To meld the soul with heart and mind,
And set the needless flesh ablaze.

The Lamb and Lion walk as one
When Heaven rolls a bleating roar,
And thievishly the Judge will pour
His blood upon the carnage spun—
And there invoke His will be done
To wrest fair souls from Satan's whips!
For those who laced His words to lips,
And kept them flowing to their death,
Will find in God eternal breath,
While evil into nothing slips.

And once the Lion's breath is felt
Within the core of Satan's spell,
God's words consume the flames of hell
As every judgment stamp is dealt.
No soul will die who prayed and knelt
Before the coming of the Lord;
But those who failed will feel His sword
As every stroke is there unleashed!
And God Almighty's reign is reached!
And all is brought to just accord!

Now Satan finds himself alone,
With not a single soul to rule—
Bereft of all his wretched drool
And every wicked flesh and bone.
God seals the gates of Hell with stone
Thrust forth by His almighty hand.
Un-worshipped will the Devil stand,
Within his empty, worthless tomb
For disobedience sealed his doom
The time he breached the Lord's command.

Lo! Lo! The time will come!
Lo! Lo! God's will be done!
Amen.

The Villanelle Master

At first, the art of writing a Villanelle seems a difficult task
to master.
The key is finding the first three lines so the rest fall into
place,
and if the Muses are kind and true, they will help you avoid
poetic disaster.

Place line 1 at lines 6, 12, and 18; so far, it's easy, no fuss,
and no fluster.
Repeat line 3 at lines 9, 15, and 19, and give your
Villanelle a shapely face!
You see! The art of writing a Villanelle is becoming less
difficult to master,

and when you practice writing a Villanelle, the words come
faster and faster.
And since line 8 rhymes with 2, 5, 11, 14, and 17—find the
words with style and grace!
Now the Muse Calliope will be more inclined to help you
avoid poetic disaster.

Failure is quick! And awfully cunning! But with a little
more work, you can outlast her!
Write, write, and write again! For in re-writing there's no
disgrace!
We know it's hard, but as you can see, the daunting
Villanelle is getting easier to master.

Find Calliope's eloquence, it is ocean vast, and
Polyhymnia's Sacredness is vaster.
Euterpe's realm sends you pleasure bound, while Majestic
Clio weaves her silk and lace.
And with their sisters, kind and true, they'll help you avoid
poetic disaster.

Give it a voice, speak from the heart, and add every
necessary tone or gesture.
Now throw it out into the waiting world! Let it ride into
the minds of the Human Race!
For in grappling with this nineteen-line poetic form, you
will become, a Villanelle Master!
And the Muses will sing! and praise your Villanelle! This
Art! This Gem! This Aster!

Thunder and Rain

The voice of the singing thunder
 Rolls across my ears,
 While the crashing rain insists
 I cater to its cheers.
 I'd never choose between the loves
 My children bring to me,
 So I'll just close my eyes a bit,
 And laud their symphony.

Touched

The moon danced brightly on Beloved's face,
And while she slept, I gently kissed her cheek.
A saline pearl escaped her eye's embrace—
It lingered, burst, and died a salty streak.

I later whispered in Beloved's ear:
"Do you, in dream, declare your heart is true?"
Beloved lightly moaned, and this I swear!
I heard her whisper back the words, "I do."

This swelled a choking tear to my own eye,
And my soul deeply drew a breath of bliss.
"Oh, Night," I sighed, "Do linger in the sky;
Accord each star the sparkle of a kiss!"

I stroked her breast, and felt my heaven move—
Such passion burns this tender flame I keep!
There, then, I prayed she burn my cheek with love,
All days, and nights, and over death's eternal sleep.

Two Gents from Wayne Township

In a boisterous bar in Wayne Township one night,
sat a fine gent--tuxedoed, red-faced, and uptight.
He yelled, "Barkeep! Two whiskeys, your best, make them neat!"
Then he guzzled one down as he rose to his feet.

When he unzipped his trousers in front of us all,
there popped out a small gent precisely a foot tall.
He zipped to the upright to tickle us pink,
and then back to the table to claim his one drink.

The barkeep in awe asked, "How'd you get such a scamp?"
Gent said, "I wished him out of this broken down lamp."
"Do you think you can treat me to one little wish?"
"It's risky," gent warned, "And not a savory dish."

Still the barkeep rubbed hard to get one million bucks,
but the million he ordered came out all in ducks.
"You're a dirty old scoundrel to do me like this!"
"You're lucky!" gent roared. "At least you're able to piss!"

Adding: "I've had the luck of a joke quite unkind.
A twelve-inch pianist? Not what I had in mind!"
Then he zipped up his gent and both hurried away,
from that boisterous bar in Wayne Township, N.J.

Wild Orchid

Beloved's ample beauties overflowed,
And stretched vivid the imagination;
And swelled natural my predilection
To nuzzle in a flower so peak endowed.

Her ravenous, moist, and biting lips threw
My soul into a river I adore,
And rabidly laid promise to outpour
The essence every orchid strives to brew.

Such sweet aching charged her musky lair!
I left her moaning lips for muted lips—
Where tongue and lips indulged in fleshy sips—
While maiden petals breathed the lusty air!

Oh! Well knew east and west Beloved's knees,
While headed north to south, my love and I!
Where forcefully we lingered, sigh for sigh,
'til frantic hips released our tortured tease.

The nectar flowed between her supple hills,
And brought her momentary peace of mind;
She quivered like a leaf inside the wind,
So tempered by the storm and heaven spills.

I—reveled in our tantalizing deaths!
But reveling brought reveling anew!
And newly my beloved sought to brew
Her nectar, stilled from passion's burning depths.

Beloved turned a Kama Sutran page—
And then another, and another still!
Until I lost control, along with will,
And noisily embraced her mounted rage!

And in the end, what more can two lives give?
But every drop of life to full extent—
The Orchid dies when Nature's dew is spent,
And spending is to conquer death—and live!

Witness to the Stations of the Cross

Jesus at Gethsemane

On the Mount of Olives praying,
Jesus looks to Heaven saying:
Father, raise this cup from me.

Though His heart is filled with sorrow,
Has He Angel strength to borrow,
For His Father's will is He.

From His face red blood is falling,
Jesus hears betrayal calling;
Knows His life is then undone.

Judas, with the soldiers creeping,
Stepping on disciples sleeping,
With a kiss betrays the Son.

Ear and Sword, in need of mending,
Knowing how His life is ending,
Jesus bids His death foretold.

All He asks is for salvation,
For the world of God's creation,
And to have His word here told.
Here His death and life unfold:

The First Station: Jesus is condemned to death

My Jesus, innocence confirms thy death,
in these, the solemn hours, when darkness reigns,
and lightless hearts bid take thy final breath.

I have found no basis—so Pilate saith,
and purifies his hands of thy blood stains.
My Lord, such purity of hand lights death.

Barabbas, freed to roam the graying heath,
is blinded by the fortune of his gains.
Now, sightless men await thy final breath.

With God above, and Satan underneath,
thy path is the path of the cleansing rains.
My Lord! My Jesus! Thy life unto death!

Thy life unto death! Words to melt the teeth!
Thy life unto death! Carried off in chains!
O heartless men—beware His final breath!

On to Golgotha! Raise thy thorny wreath!
No golden crown shall free thee of thy pains!
My Jesus, innocence confirms thy death
when faithless men exact thy final breath!

The Second Station: Jesus Carries His Cross

My Lord, thy limbs embrace the nail and wood,
and on thy shoulders press the sins of Man—
of thine own will. My Lord, how is this good?

Where lives divinity in flesh and blood?
Are men to darken light thy Will began?
Man, my Lord, forges nails, thy Will the wood!

Such heavy, heavy pains thy flesh withstood!
Heavier still these sins thou wrest from Satan.
I ask, Lord, how is this for thine own good?—

Burdens, plied by eyeless men, men who would
see thee fall short beneath the timbered span,
and long to see my Lord bear nail and wood.

Why art thou, Son of Man, misunderstood?
How shall my sins serve God's eternal plan?
Of thine own will, my Lord, for my own good?

If any man should stand where thou hast stood,
shall he cross the path the Son of God began?
Let us pray thy limbs succumb to nail and wood,
For thy Father waits, O Lord, and God is good.

The Third Station: Jesus Falls the First Time

Almighty God, thou art conscious of all,
and thy Son, as Man, knows the flesh is weak.
Forgive us, Lord, for we stumble and fall.

Help us resist the Devil should he call
us, and let us not listen to him speak.
Save us, God almighty, conscious of all!

Lift from our backs Satan's heavy pall.
Make thy light eternal the star we seek.
And forgive us, Lord—we stumble and fall.

Purify our hearts, thoughts, and our limbs shall
transport the timber to Golgotha's peak.
Thou art God, Almighty, and Mover of all.

Give us courage, strength, so we may stand tall,
even on this day, when the hours are bleak.
We hurt (my Lord) when we stumble and fall.

We shall kneel before thee and thy Words recall!
For thy glory belongs to those humble and meek!
Thou art God! Almighty! Conscious of all!
And thy hand is outstretched when we stumble and fall.

The Fourth Station: Jesus Meets His Mother

O blesséd Mary, heart full of sorrow,
Thy Son, Jesus, aches for thy soothing hand,
and thy healing kiss upon His brow.

In His eyes wells the agony that calls to thee now,
but the path He takes is not thine to command—
O blesséd Mother, full of His sorrow.

Thy womb knew grace, thou felt Him grow.
Thou brought Him forth—flesh of thy flesh—and
thy breath often cooled the warmth of His brow.

Now His flesh is torn, and His head hangs low,
and He knows in His heart thou understand—
thy sorrow, O Mother, is also His sorrow.

Mother! Mother! Let thy burning tears flow!
Let thy grief be known throughout the land.
And cherish days past when thou kissed His brow.

Thy Son suffers today for the sake of tomorrow.
He shall have the glory Our Father hath planned.
Yet, grieving Mother, greatest is thy sorrow,
For a crown of thorns torments His brow.

The Fifth Station: Simon helps Jesus Carry His Cross

Take unto thyself, Simon of Cyrene,
The cross that shall bare to the world thy name,
And thy heart to Jesus the Nazarene.

Thy footsteps, guided by the Hand Unseen,
shall take thee through the path of sorrowful fame,
for His cross is thine, good Simon of Cyrene.

Thy kinsmen shall suffer all thou hath seen,
felt, heard; and cursed or blest, thou shalt proclaim—
thy life belongs to Jesus the Nazarene.

Though His limbs tremble so, He is faith serene,
with a spirit as pure as the burning flame.
Help thy Lord Jesus, Simon of Cyrene—

walk with Him, give Him thy shoulder to lean
on, and light shall ever be thine own frame
when thou art touched by Jesus, the Nazarene.

For the sake of the world thou must intervene.
His path and thy path are one and the same.
Take His cross unto thyself, Simon of Cyrene,
for He is Lord Jesus Christ…the Divine Nazarene.

The Sixth Station: Veronica Wipes the Face of Jesus

Thou knelt before Jesus, fear in thy soul,
When thou touched His robe to ease thy pain.
For thy faith, Veronica, He made thee whole.

Now His face is broken, His wounds are foul,
The crowd looks upon Him with great disdain.
Yet, go thou unto Jesus—no fear in thy soul.

For thy soothing eyes that His heart console,
thy simple cloth shall His countenance gain.
Remember, Veronica, He made thee whole.

Give Him the reverence faithless men stole.
Impress with thy veil so His blood doth stain
it, and there gaze upon Jesus, Heart of thy soul.

Blessed be His face the faithful extol,
and the purest who follow His glory attain,
for the faithful, Veronica, He shall take whole.

Let His journey continue, and the death knell toll,
For Our Father in Heaven must see Him again!
Thou knelt before Jesus, a penitent soul,
And for this, Veronica, He made thee whole.

The Seventh Station: Jesus Falls the Second Time

Once more, O Lord, the Tempter weighs thee down
and promises to ease Thy aching heart.
He is envious and seeks Thy thorn-laden crown!

Sorely he craves Thy glory for his own.
Sore are the favors he feigns to impart.
Again, Lord Jesus, the Tempter weighs Thee down!

Because heavy and weary Thy flesh hast grown
the Tempter endeavors to see Thee part
with Thy envious, glorious, thorn-laden crown!

The Dark One's dominion to Thee is known,
but Thy faith in Thy Father shall shake it apart—
though anew, my Lord, the Tempter weighs Thee down!

Those ruled by sin in Thy Light shall drown,
O Jesus, for Thou art…
my Saviour and Lord of the thorn-laden crown.

Now let men weep o'er the seeds they hath sown
and by thine own words maketh the Devil depart.
When the Great Tempter seeks to weigh thee down,
Lord, give unto us—thy thorn-laden crown!

The Eighth Station: Jesus Speaks to the Women of Jerusalem

Weep, Daughters of Jerusalem—weep!
Nary a tear for His suffering sake,
but for thine own and thy children's keep!

Wail, wail for the shepherdless sheep
that slumber in the field while the Wolf is awake!
Weep, Daughters of Jerusalem—weep!

But not for the Lord whose wounds are deep!
But for thy brethren who the Lamb forsake.
Yes, weep for thine own, and thy children's keep!

Thou shalt bless the sister whose womb doth sleep
for truly thy children of thy sins partake.
O, weep, Daughters of Jerusalem—weep!

Thy path to Heaven is now long and steep,
for the City of God, like His heart, shall break!
Weep for thine own and thy children's keep!

O Daughters of Jerusalem, weep...
but not a tear for His suffering sake.
Weep, Daughters of Jerusalem, weep.
Weep for thine own and thy children's keep.

The Ninth Station: Jesus Falls the Third Time

My Lord, though thy flesh three times hast failed thee,
and the crowd yet clamors for thy crucifixion,
still, thou riseth, O humble man from Galilee.

Gone are the olive branches of Gethsemane.
Thy wooden cross is now the source of thy affliction.
And it burns thy flesh which three times hast failed thee.

Is it for the love of the man who bends his knee,
or the sake of one woman's act of contrition,
that thou still riseth, O humble man of Galilee?

Truly, my sins are contrary to thy sanctity,
and my soul is not worthy of thy benediction,
for my flesh as well many times hast failed thee.

Thou knowest the way to quell thine own agony,
Yet thy flesh endures for the sake of my salvation,
and anew thou riseth, O humble man of Galilee.

But Golgotha waits for the final catastrophe.
It is there where all shall come to fruition.
For though thy flesh three times hast failed thee,
yet thou riseth, O humblest of men, man of Galilee.

The Tenth Station: Jesus is stripped of His Garments

Lord, not a thing on Earth to Heaven rises.
No bird, not gold, nor any vesture worn,
but the soul...divested of its guises.

Foolish are these men, their earthly vices.
They strip Thee to nakedness reborn—
but nothing of the flesh to Heaven rises.

Lots the sinners cast for earthly prizes.
Thy garments, from thy body roughly torn,
leave Thy flesh divested of its guises.

Poverty is what the flesh despises.
But poverty is but an earthly thorn,
and not a thing of earth to Heaven rises.

Thou maketh for my sake all sacrifices
and indignities so grave Thy flesh hast borne
so my soul may be freed of all its guises.

The man who feels thy agony and cries is
the man whom all of Earth shall come to mourn.
For not a thing on Earth to Heaven rises
but the boundless soul...stripped of all disguises.

The Eleventh Station: Jesus is nailed to the cross

Cruel nails hammered through thy hands and feet,
a crown of thorns, and Thy flesh aflame
prepare Thee, Jesus, for Thy end to meet.

The Wolf now prowls around the lambs that bleat
while callous men move to maul and maim—
by hammering nails through thy hands and feet.

Thy blood gushes forth with each pounding beat.
They number Thy bones and curse Thy name.
Arrange Thyself, Lord, for Thy end to meet.

Thy agony burns to a frenzied heat
as cruel men seek to break thy frame—
by hammering nails through thy hands and feet.

The fierce ringing irons thy flesh maltreat—
they gouge, pierce, to a murderous game.
Prepare Thyself, Lord, for Thy end to meet.

Thy path is the path that is soon complete,
and because of Thy cross the world shall claim:
Cruel nails hammered through thy hands and feet,
Prepared Thee, Jesus, for Thy end to meet.

The Twelfth Station: Jesus dies on the cross

From His cross the Saviour cried—
to commend to God His soul.
Then because He loved He died.

Scourged and mocked, then crucified,
some, His anguish, did condole—
others laughed when Jesus cried!

Were forgiven, those who lied.
What was broken He made whole.
So He loved. And so He died.

Oh the weight! The crashing tide!
From bruised lips His last breath stole,
when Lord Jesus bled and cried.

Nail and hammer Christ defied.
With His wounds He paid His toll
showing us for love He died.

O'er my life let God preside.
If I weep, may Christ console.
From His cross the Saviour cried.
For our sins the Lord hath died.

Thirteenth Station: Jesus is taken down from the cross

The pure and good our God to Earth hath sent
is taken from the cross that sealed His fate,
and laid in Mary's arms—His life well spent.

No longer shall fiery thorns torment,
the physical anguish, nor Death await,
the pure and good our God to Earth hath sent.

The world doth tremble and comes to lament
our innocent Jesus, pure and sedate,
now laid in Mary's arms; His life well spent.

Behold the Son of Man! His body bent.
Behold! The Son of God! How came Man to hate
the pure and good our God to Earth hath sent?

Weeping Mother—thy heart a sword hath rent,
and there it shall stay, never to abate,
for He lies in thine arms, His life well spent.

Thunderously bellows Our Father's firmament!
And Seraphs gather at Heaven's Gate!
They await the pure and good our God to Earth hath sent,
now cradled in His Mother's arms…His life all spent.

The Fourteenth Station: Jesus is laid in the sepulcher

O grieving Mary, of the blesséd womb,
thine arms bear the blood of our God divine,
and the flesh that longs for His Earthly tomb.

If thy heart is shrouded by sorrow's gloom—
thy Son is the light that shall ever shine,
O weeping Mary of the blesséd womb.

A veil of sorrow may over us loom,
but all moves according to God's design,
and our Savior longs for His Earthly tomb.

As Seraphim gather, and our censers fume,
all lives and deaths shall intertwine.
O grieving Mary, of the blesséd womb—

plant thy progeny! So His flower may bloom,
so His flesh may feed, and His blood make wine
of the Christ—who longs for His Earthly tomb.

The rock and the soil now wait to consume
the flesh in thine arms of our God divine.
O grieving Mary, of the blesséd womb,
Accord thy son, Jesus, his Earthly tomb.

The Third Day: The Resurrection of Jesus Christ

Hallelujah, O Lord! Thou art the Risen One!
The sting of Death holds no dominion over thee,
And because of thy resurrection, God's will is done!

Thou art man of Heaven, divine begotten Son,
Raised from the tomb by Thy Father's decree.
Hallelujah! My Lord Jesus! Thou art the Risen One!

The battle over darkness by thy light is won!
Unto Thee praises, for over Death is thy Victory!
And because of thy Resurrection, God's will is done!

The sacred tomb is empty, Thy transformation begun,
And Thou art elevated over thy pains at Calvary.
Hail and Hallelujah, O Lord, Thou art the Risen One!

Thou hast changed the dreadful night into the morning Sun,
And within Thy spirit lives all of life's mystery!
Hail to God, O Jesus, His will in thee is done!

Those who turn away shall in Death find oblivion!
Those who follow Thee shall bask in Thy glory!
Hallelujah! Lord Jesus! Thou art the Risen One!
And by thy resurrection, God's will hath been done!

Life after Death

Into hell our Lord descended,
To give life to those suspended
In the turmoil of the night.

Then to Heaven's gate ascending,
Jesus grants them, never-ending,
God's forgiving, loving light.

All who seek Him find His blessing;
Every soul, in sin distressing,
If repentant, hath reply.

Over Death our Lord's victorious,
In His Kingdom sits He glorious,
None with faith in Him shall die.

His own flesh and blood He offered,
For our sake and sins He suffered,
Yet He gained eternal breath.

When my eyes by sleep are taken,
May the Lord my spirit waken
Far above the veil of death.

Amen—Witness of the Stations of the Cross—Amen.

Haiku

A spotless white Dove
Out of blue sky dives the Hawk
and lands on her wings

A summer night's kiss
Comet through the Milky Way
takes our breaths away

Bear tracks in the snow
Pine trees heading for the hills
hopping on one leg

Beauty in the morgue
Wild animals in the streets
People in the zoo

Bolero rhythm
Pair of motionless dancers
Synchronized heartbeats

Bookstore mother drinks
hot tea at twenty thousand leagues
Kids home with their dad

Candlelight dinner
The awakening Orchid
opens its petals

Caressing fingers
Cheeks in the palms of my hands
burning while we kiss

Dancing on the bed
A meteorite shower
under the new moon

Demure and petite
lady Jekylls and Hydes it
The Tigress pounces

Feathery fingers
playing delicate music
Ripples in a pond

Flame inside a flame
Candle crying waxen tears
A dazzling demise

Hint of Drakkar Noir
over the scent of Poison
Dripping Poison Noir

Lady in green sweats
Scarlet Tanager in love
singing by the road

Midnight rendezvous
Sharing of forbidden fruits
Apple cores remain

Moon over ocean
A sigh riding over waves
of silken tresses

Parallel railroads
traveling in the moonlight
A ship hurries by

Parade of snowflakes
Popping corn in the fireplace
spring onto the rug

Petals on the floor
Fireworks in satin sheets
toasting little death

Scarlet Tanager
sitting on the railroad tracks
drinking from the snow

Slithering rattler
An igloo lost in the snow
feels the summer heat

Sparrow in the wind
Oak trees bow to the sunset
falling on the graveyard

Tangential glances
Wine-red lips drinking water
intoxicate me

Under the full moon
Lightning bugs interpreting
each constellation

Under the full moon
Two Lambada silhouettes
shake the candle's light

Whispering Orchid
I stopped to share her secret
and she died with me

Widow dressed in black
Suitor trembling at the door
hanging by a thread

Winter's icy breath
Silver moonbeams burn Autumn
with their frigid hands

Café Espresso at the Border

The travelers come from miles around and distant lands.
They whisper noisily, moving past the espresso machine—
an essential locomotive—hissing and ceasing, hissing and
ceasing, while Mozart streams down from the heavens.
And I, a voyager in a settlement of voyagers, seek solace.

I stake my solitary claim at the corner table, And I am
alone with the aromas fleeing from the black bullets with
the silver casings. I am alone by choice as I watch an old
geezer give his lady a young man's wink.

The Gothic maiden, multi-pierced of lip and brow,
flaunts her tattooed arms. The nuts-and-bolts aficionado
behind the register gawks at her presence. In the distance,
at the magazine rack, the pimpled lad sneaks a peek at the
naked babes.

At the other end, the three-quarter-aged fellow openly
admires their nude perfection. Nearby, the grandmother
discreetly inquires the whereabouts of the restrooms, and
her four-year-old granddaughter proudly yells out,
"Number one and number two!" Meanwhile, the dark-gray,
pin-stripe suit is all business with Baron's.

The caravan stops momentarily, and there is an air of
Evian, café latte, mint tea, chocolate chip, nuts and bolts,
pimples, whispers, and winks, while the Gothic maiden's
red-eyed black skull, above the crossed bones, eyes us all.

Suddenly, a chilled brunette rushes in and sits at the table
across from me. The mist rises from the paper cup as it

touches her lips-she moans, and melts! New Balance
weights come off, and like long lost lovers, her grateful
dogs caress.

No invitation is forthcoming, or outgoing, as our eyes
shake hands, our heads nod, we smile, and her gaze falls
peacefully, hungrily to a page in the middle of her book;
and a consoling thought enters my mind like a knowing
whisper from her smacking lips: I am alone, by choice, and
I am not alone.

Faith

I sit on the edge of a precipice wondering why
my trust is far, far stronger than I
and the rope is no thicker than a strand of hair,
yet I'm asked to take a leap out there.

Can I trust my heart and dare believe?
Is my vision true or do my eyes deceive?
I need to find out, and so—
here I go.

In Retrospect

To be untrue to self is to fail self.
Will you place your book on an empty shelf?
Which impostor looks in the mirror and sees
The impostor who fails in all degrees.

To truly love is to become unquestionable.
To fly high and be truly free is to become irreproachable.
To believe in Truth is to become indestructible.

What then shall I become?

Will I be two or will I be one?
Will I be taken from the shelf?
Or will they take my other self?

I *will* find out next time I look
into the glass that holds my book,
And I'll smash myself to bits and see
Is it him or is it me?

Juxtaposition

Love is:

light
a bell
an aroma
spoken
felt,

willingly losing
heart
mind
and soul.

Hate is:

All of the above

minus

Love is.

Nightingale at My Window

A Nightingale lands
on a branch outside
my open window
one sunny morning.

I offer water,
food, an open hand,
but she doesn't budge,
and she remains silent.

I speak kindly, softly, and not a note.

I ask:
What ails you?
Have I offended you?

When I move away from the window
she turns her head
as if to keep an eye on me.

She waits.

Feeling rejected, I begin to sing
a melancholy song.

She flutters to my windowsill,
settles down, closes her eyes…
and listens.

Shallow Graves

Hampton, my five-year old daughter's hamster,
died one winter just before the snow arrived.
I placed him in a matchbox filled with wood
shavings from his bed, and buried
him near the farthest border of our garden.

Hampton knew nothing
about considerations for the dead, and the crow
that dug him up proceeded to eat him.
The crow cawed its thanks,
much to the chagrin of my daughter,
who came screaming to tell me.

I should have dug a deeper grave, I thought,
after my next few words took my daughter's mind off
Hampton.
(Sometimes, death goes easier with ice cream and cake).
And now, my daughter knows why
people are buried six feet deep.

As for me, I'd rather feed the crows and his friends,
since I'll have nothing to hide, and considerations
for the dead will be of no concern to me when I'm gone.

Stigmata

The Emergency Room reeks of something.
It's hard to tell what, when I'm impressed with thorns.
And the pain in my palms, my crippled feet—
when will it go away?
Now my side hurts, and I'm thirsty.

I'm looking for the Angel of Death
while others run away from him.
But who will he find first?
It's rhetorical.
After all, I'll soon be thirty-three.

Oh, what fools we are!
What do the sick and dying know of suffering?
What do the doctors know of suffering?
What do I know of suffering?
It's not my pain I feel.

The nurse calls me in—
I have to get to the delivery room.
An only child there waits for me.
He reaches out for me.
I get to hold him.
I need to hold him.
I hold him so tightly he dies in my arms,
and now I'm better, at least for a little while.

Oh, yes, I can smell it now—
the open wounds on my back.

The Dance

I met near my small village, on a sandy beach, a pale woman who was an ocean. My dark little sea, she said, I've walked a thousand years for you to be with me, and I have brought the stars upon my shoulders to light the way. Then she asked me to dance.

My dread transformed me into a rock, and so she evolved into a mountain. I was soon a seedling, and so she proffered a garden. I hid in a puff of smoke, and so she engulfed me in a cloud. When I sprouted wings to escape, she afforded me the wind, tossing me into the roiling waters, where I became as she.

Thereafter, my strides became miles. In seconds, I was upon the next village in my journey, a thousand years hence.

Lined up beyond the sand, the concrete forest stood tall and proud, dripping with silver and gold. There I saw and walked towards a familiar face. Moquette was smiling, standing at the doorway to her humble abode, and I saw no fear in those dark-brown eyes. So I walked in, moved towards the center of the room, and I lifted one arm in the air, the other I placed over my hip. It was time to dance.

The Eyes of War

Run! Innocent child, from War's imminent disaster!
Hide from the limb eliminator.
Flee his sanity-siphoning roar, his womb-fruit
demolishing,
and avert your gaze from his bloodshot eyes—
they are the great annihilator of souls!

Run! Innocent child, from War's tyrannical disaster!
Flee the ravager, who destroys his mother's womb.
Dig your trenches six-feet deep,
dig more trenches six-feet deep,
and shed your tears upon her bones.

Run! Innocent child, from War's human disaster!
Run into the settled dust, the flameless ash,
and find the stone that marks my grave,
and place a purple orchid there,
to let me know you thought of me.

Run! Innocent child, freed from disaster!—
across green grass my flesh has fed.
And if my death's a soldier's song,
then I have paved a peaceful road,
and plucked the treacherous eyes of War!

Tuning Fork

"I wager, Truth, that I can strike a chord,
in any key, more soothing to the ear.
My notes are varied, rightly placed upon
the scale, and bluntly roll on past the tongue,
through teeth so tight, and lips so loosely pursed,
they ride the wind more often than the clouds,
and need not be arranged, nor tuned, just played!"

"O Lies, I need not take the wager for
inside me rings the two-prong tuning fork.
When tapped, its single song, so pure and true,
though called to set the rest, is seldom heard.
 When tapped, the ear will hear its voice and call
it flat, preferring deafness to the sharp,
resounding echo of one crystal note!

 "But tapped, again, no other note will sound
except my own, and you can keep it up,
both day and night, the painful, tapping beat,
to no avail, for I must sing the note
which will be heard when all of yours have died!"

Unanswered Questions

Exhilarating were the moments
of confident desire,
the fiery, inebriating words
of the most glorious of all emotions,
and my heart found solace
behind their blinding mist.

Then the blinding mist,
like a cataract, grew thicker and
it took from me a little,
then a little more,
and then finally all.

The words, once a crashing tide,
a raging river, lava spewing out of
an impassioned volcano, drowned in some abyss
beneath an unknown sea.

Sometimes, there are colder things beating
within the core of human flesh
than are swimming within
the deepest trenches
of the darkest of oceans.

What I Have Learned

Pain and sorrow can
be replaced by things unsought.
There is a storm
within the warmest of eyes.
There is a life-giving force
behind the gentlest of lips.
And if one dares anew,
one can sink into that storm,
breathe,
and live again.

THE END

www.ingramcontent.com/pod-product-compliance
Lightning Source LLC
LaVergne TN
LVHW021525080426
835509LV00018B/2671